This Journal Belongs to:

_____

_____

_____

_____

Fonts used:
Honey Florist Font - E-Pub License, License number: 3829
Enactment Date 21/02/2022, Licensor Typhoon TypeTM by Suthi Srisopha

INTRODUCTION

From journaling to collective prayers, there are many creative ways to practice prayer. Keeping a prayer journal can influence your overall well-being. It can help you cope with stressful times, gain strength to avoid temptation and find direction in your life. Prayer can also help you learn more about God's plan for you and your life.

Are you struggling to discover your purpose in this world? Your loving Heavenly Father wants you to communicate with Him as much as possible. The best way to communicate with God is through prayer? Prayer will give you important knowledge of God's loving nature. It can help you better understand your purpose and provide the emotional foundation for a sense of purpose and meaning in life. Numerous studies have proven that the experience of prayer makes us feel connected to something larger than ourselves. However, it's not enough to just feel like you have a meaningful life; you also need to feel driven to make a positive impact on this world.

10 Scientifically Proven Benefits of Prayer

From health benefits to higher self-esteem and positive thinking, there are numerous benefits of prayer. In general, you will become a lot more content with your life by practicing prayer. It is scientifically proven that the human brain has a built-in bias that causes us to focus on negativity. There is an evolutionary reason that is intended to alert you to possible danger, forcing you to live with a constant survival mode mentality. When your brain experiences "threats" in your social environment, your cognitive functions are changing. It causes you to over-focus on negativity, making you easily distracted and afraid. It decreases analytic thinking, creativity, and problem-solving abilities. Cultivating prayer as a way of life is one of the best ways to overcome drama, negative thoughts, and stressful situations. Daily prayer and prayer journals can bring stillness and peace into your life. There are 10 benefits of prayer. They can include:

• Reducing negative emotions. Prayer could keep the person calm and centered, focusing on words that described the nature of God.

• Gaining a new perspective on stressful situations. Feeling loved and supported may help with managing stress and anxiety.

• Reducing or eliminating medical conditions. Prayer is beneficial with conditions such as depression, heart diseases, chronic pain, insomnia, high blood pressure, anxiety, and so forth. Religion and prayer give patients a sense of meaning and peace, so they cope more effectively with their conditions. A significant number of studies have shown a correlation between prayer practice and lower blood pressure, reduced risk of diabetes, and heart diseases. It can help people cope with chronic illness.

• Increasing self-awareness. When you focus on being in God's presence, He will help you see yourself and your whole life through His unconditional love and acceptance. It will significantly increase your self-awareness and God-awareness.

• Increasing imagination and creativity. We are creative beings; it's important that we understand who our source is and what it looks like. Remember – God is the only one that can help you tap into the creative power! If you review each day with thanksgiving and reflection, if you ask for guidance and grace, your creativity grows and develops day by day. Corinthians - "No eye has seen, no ear has heard, and no mind has imagined what God has prepared for those who love him."

• Increasing patience and tolerance. Patience and tolerance are hard in this hectic world. Don't worry, God understands that. He can help you gain the power to renew your patience and strength. That's where prayer comes into play.

• Reducing anger and aggression. When you pray, you're focused on positive emotions, gratitude, and forgiveness. Remember, there's plenty of love in the world and you deserve it. That's where generosity comes into play!

• Becoming more forgiving. We all want to feel deeply connected to others, secure, and fully appreciated by them. Forgiveness is associated with better relationships, understanding, and satisfaction with life.

• Protecting you against temptation. Studies have shown that people who practice prayer are half as likely to use drugs, compared to non-religious people. Plus, children and teens who are involved in spiritual activities have better educational results.

• Increasing financial satisfaction. Many studies have shown that people who hold and practice prayer with a positive outlook have a better financial position, compared to non-religious people. In fact, prayer can improve your financial health by helping you to spend your money mindfully and build good money habits.

HOW TO INCREASE THE POWER OF YOUR PRAYERS

Regular Fasting

"...and then was a widow until she was eighty-four. She never left the temple but worshiped night and day, fasting and praying." – Luke 2:37. Jesus Christ fasted for 40 days and 40 nights before in the wilderness to endure temptation from Satan. After those 40 days, the devil disappeared, and "angels came and attended him".

When we pray and fast, we feel closer to our Heavenly Father, like Jesus did. Plus, it helps us clear our minds and understand certain things God wants us to do. If you have a sense of deep spiritual hunger, desperately seeking the Word of God, prayer will help you listen to God's voice. It means that you might understand God's message of salvation that the first followers of Jesus proclaimed to people. When you are deprived of food for a certain period of time, your physical body will weaken, but God's Word will become your spiritual food, strengthening your spirit and body. As we can die physically without food, we can die spiritually without God's Word. And so it is!

Using the Bible

Use your Prayer journal and Holy Books to become part of God's covenant. It will help you learn God's commandments, which are the most important principles of life. Study and follow commandments and try to apply them to all life situations. Bible verses offer helpful and wise ideas, answering your prayers and keeping your life free of problems. And most importantly, they keep you closely connected to your Heavenly Father.

Thank God

When you pray, thank God for the blessings you receive. Thank God even when times are difficult. It is not always easy, but thankfulness opens the gates of heaven! Remember, grateful people, are happy people! One of the most important keys to a more powerful prayer life is to appreciate God's will by honoring him through daily actions. Respect God's will with absolute certainty, and His arms will be the safest place where you can be!

Always say what you need

Saying what you want is a powerful tool to get what you want! As simple as that! Our Heavenly Father insists we ask for help, not because He needs to know everything, but because He respects our desires. You are free to choose; you are free to ask and not to ask. The decision is all yours. You can lift your face to see the Lord in the darkest moments, you can lift your voice to call out to His divine voice. You can simply say, "God, help me!". Please speak about your needs directly and honestly; He is always ready to respond to your needs! Help will come in a certain way.

Praying for others in need

Every prayer has power. Prayer for other people has enormous power. Jesus is praying for each of us at every moment. If you are worried about your beloved one or your friend, keep in mind that Jesus called the weak to come to him for peace. Prayer will release anxiety, help you find a solution for problems, and bring you peace of mind!

Forgive

Prayer brings you towards forgiveness. We all make mistakes. If you seek forgiveness from someone or you should forgive someone, turn to God's wisdom and ask Him for help. When we pray for forgiveness, we are able to not only receive forgiveness but give forgiveness to others in return. Resentment is a toxic emotion. Forgiveness helps you overcome resentment and heal your heart, body, and soul. The fastest way to forgive or receive forgiveness is by practicing prayers.

HOW TO USE THIS
PRAYER JOURNAL?

Carve out time to reflect and incorporate journaling in your daily routine. You can write your prayer journal first thing in the morning or just before bed at night. However, it's important to put it into your daily schedule. It is also important to keep this book with you wherever you go! Even if you don't write in it, you'll have it for a godly inspiration in everyday activities. It's also a good reminder of God's love and acceptance!

One more tip – If you practice prayer at the same time every day, you can easily get into the habit of doing it. If you are confused and full of emotions, do not worry; start small and think big. Keeping prayer journal forces you to think about positive aspects. The more you practice prayer, the more you'll notice things that we usually overlook. When "small" things like electricity in your house become an object of gratitude, your journey to enlightenment begins. Remember ¬– God always listens to you; He always provides the answers and guidance you seek; He answers your prayers in the form of feelings, thoughts, scriptures, or the actions of others. He wants us to pour out our hearts in union with Him and His son! May God bless you, your family, and your friends!

God hears your heart

This is the confidence we have in approaching God: that if we ask anything according to his will, he hears us. And if we know that he hears us — whatever we ask — we know that we have what we asked of him.

John 5:14-15

GOD LISTENS TO YOU

God listens when you pray with a pure heart. A life with God is a journey; it is exciting and adventurous, but it is also filled with challenges. Prayer will help you stay close to God no matter what, even when you are not sure if God is listening to you. Remember, He always has your best in mind.

Your first task is to roll up your sleeves, grab your Holy Bible, a blank piece of paper, and a pen. Write a letter to God.

Reflections and thoughts

_____

_____

_____

_____

_____

_____

_____

I am grateful for

_____

_____

_____

_____

_____

_____

Things on my mind

_____

_____

_____

_____

_____

_____

Prayer requests

_____

_____

_____

_____

_____

Prayers answered

_____

_____

_____

_____

_____

God hears your heart

The Lord will keep you from all harm — He will watch over your life; the Lord will watch over your coming and going both now and forevermore.

Psalm 121:7-8

GOD'S INFLUENCE

God always watches over you as you go through life. Give Him your full devotion and you will experience an amazing influence of His divine reward. On the other hand, God respects our freedom and our choices. He loves us unconditionally, and true love can never be forced.

If you turn to God and tell him, "I trust you and I surrender!", God will respond to you. Do you want to ask God for something?

Reflections and thoughts

_____

_____

_____

_____

_____

_____

_____

_____

I am grateful for

_____

_____

_____

_____

_____

_____

Things on my mind

_____

_____

_____

_____

_____

_____

Prayer requests

_____

_____

_____

_____

_____

_____

Prayers answered

_____

_____

_____

_____

_____

_____

God hears your heart

You have searched me, LORD, and you know me. You know when I sit and when I rise; you perceive my thoughts from afar. You discern my going out and my lying down; you are familiar with all my ways. Before a word is on my tongue you, LORD, know it completely.

Psalm 139:1-4

GOD KNOWS YOU

God knows everything, including your wishes, your fears, and deep aspirations. God always hears you; He knows you and your very deepest emotions – more than you ever could. Remember, we are really known and loved by God!

Open your mind, turn your hands up to the sky, and with pure heart say to God, "I believe that you know my deepest need. I am aware of my limitations and weaknesses, trusting that you are always working for my good." What else would you say to God?

Reflections and thoughts

_____
_____
_____
_____
_____
_____
_____
_____

I am grateful for

_____
_____
_____
_____
_____
_____

Things on my mind

_____
_____
_____
_____
_____
_____

Prayer requests

_____
_____
_____
_____
_____
_____

Prayers answered

_____
_____
_____
_____
_____
_____

God hears your heart

If I regard iniquity in my heart, the Lord will not hear me: But verily God hath heard me; he hath attended to the voice of my prayer. Blessed be God, which hath not turned away my prayer or his mercy from me.

Psalm 66:18-20

LISTENING TO THE VOICE OF GOD

Just ten to fifteen minutes of listening time not only adds a huge dose of stillness to your everyday life but you will gain a better understanding, knowledge, and wisdom. How to do that?

Do not let your mind race and jump to various distractions. Just take a few deep breaths and close your eyes; then, focus on God's voice alone. What did you hear?

Reflections and thoughts

_____

_____

_____

_____

_____

_____

_____

I am grateful for

_____

_____

_____

_____

_____

_____

Things on my mind

_____

_____

_____

_____

_____

_____

Prayer requests

_____

_____

_____

_____

_____

_____

Prayers answered

_____

_____

_____

_____

_____

_____

God hears your heart

What do you know that we do not know?
What do you understand that we do not?

Job 15:9

ASK FOR GUIDANCE

Whatever you are looking for, keep in mind that God can help you. There is nothing impossible for God! If you have fallen on difficult times, just take a breath and talk to the Lord. Give Him your troubles, ask for guidance, rely on His wisdom and mercy. Pour out your heart, God can handle anything.

The exercise for this week is – I am really struggling with… Write it down.

Reflections and thoughts

_____

_____

_____

_____

_____

_____

_____

_____

I am grateful for

_____

_____

_____

_____

_____

Things on my mind

_____

_____

_____

_____

_____

Prayer requests

_____

_____

_____

_____

_____

Prayers answered

_____

_____

_____

_____

_____

God hears your heart

Therefore, you also must be ready, for in an hour when you least expect, the Son of Man is coming.

Matthew 24:24

ARE YOU READY?

The Holy book reminds us over and over again of the peace that comes from being loved by God. There are good and bad times and they are all part of God's plan for us. Pray for a close relationship with the Lord. Prayer is one of the most powerful ways to connect with God.

Remember, God will never abandon you. How about you? Are you ready to believe?

Reflections and thoughts

_____
_____
_____
_____
_____
_____
_____
_____

I am grateful for

_____
_____
_____
_____
_____
_____

Things on my mind

_____
_____
_____
_____
_____
_____

Prayer requests

_____
_____
_____
_____
_____
_____

Prayers answered

_____
_____
_____
_____
_____
_____

Praying for others

Therefore, confess your sins to each other and pray for each other so that you may be healed. The prayer of a righteous person is powerful and effective.

James 5:16

WHAT IS THE IMPORTANCE OF PRAYING FOR OTHERS?

When you pray, the Lord works through your heart, using your humble thoughts to align your mind to His will. It makes your life peaceful and fulfilling. In this way, you are creating a positive impact every day. If you love a person, but you can't help him/her, you can always pray for them.

Write a list of people to pray for.

Reflections and thoughts

_____

_____

_____

_____

_____

_____

_____

I am grateful for

_____

_____

_____

_____

_____

_____

Things on my mind

_____

_____

_____

_____

_____

_____

Prayer requests

_____

_____

_____

_____

_____

Prayers answered

_____

_____

_____

_____

_____

Praying for others

Therefore, confess your sins to each other and pray for each other so that you may be healed. The prayer of a righteous person is powerful and effective.

James 5:16

WHAT IS THE IMPORTANCE OF PRAYING FOR OTHERS?

When you pray, the Lord works through your heart, using your humble thoughts to align your mind to His will. It makes your life peaceful and fulfilling. In this way, you are creating a positive impact every day. If you love a person, but you can't help him/her, you can always pray for them.

Write a list of people to pray for.

Reflections and thoughts

_____

_____

_____

_____

_____

_____

_____

_____

I am grateful for

_____

_____

_____

_____

_____

Things on my mind

_____

_____

_____

_____

_____

Prayer requests

_____

_____

_____

_____

_____

Prayers answered

_____

_____

_____

_____

_____

Praying for others

Is anyone among you sick? Then he must call for the elders of the church and they are to pray over him, anointing him with oil in the name of the Lord.

James 5:14

THE POWER OF PRAYING FOR ONE ANOTHER

Praying for others is our privilege. It is a true blessing! Praying for others unites us in a community, lightens our burdens, and focuses us on kindness and compassion. Praying for others gets our focus off of ourselves, transforming our soul from selfishness to altruism. Praying for others is a good source of healing; it can heal your body and soul. When Jesus Christ was praying for his friends and enemies alike, He prayed for their faith and against temptations.

The Holy book encourages us to pray for everything we want. For instance: Lord, help my friend to find a job, give him good health…
Continue the list…

Reflections and thoughts

_____

_____

_____

_____

_____

_____

_____

_____

I am grateful for

_____

_____

_____

_____

_____

_____

Things on my mind

_____

_____

_____

_____

_____

_____

Prayer requests

_____

_____

_____

_____

_____

Prayers answered

_____

_____

_____

_____

_____

Praying for others

Is anyone among you suffering? Let him pray. Is anyone cheerful? Let him sing praise.

James 5:13

PRAYING FOR FAMILY

There are many ways to pray for your close family and immediate family. In this week of prayer, you can pray for each member individually. For instance, pray for children on Monday, seek God's help in keeping your parents pure in thought and deed on Tuesday, pray for your spouse on Wednesday, and so on. You can pray for all of them every single day. On the other hand, you can pray for your children throughout the week. For instance, pray for their health on Monday, ask for God's hand of protection (physical, emotional, and spiritual) on Tuesday, and pray for their faith on Wednesday.

Make time each day to talk to God and give Him your worries and fears about family. What will you say to God?

Reflections and thoughts

_____

_____

_____

_____

_____

_____

_____

I am grateful for

_____

_____

_____

_____

_____

Things on my mind

_____

_____

_____

_____

_____

Prayer requests

_____

_____

_____

_____

_____

Prayers answered

_____

_____

_____

_____

_____

Praying for others

When Job prayed for his friends, the LORD restored his fortunes, giving him twice as much as before!

Job 42:10

PRAYING FOR FRIENDS

When your friend is going through really tough times, you suffer along with him/her. You can reach out to your friend with your moral support and financial help, but never underestimate the power of prayer. Whether your friend is dealing with a serious disease, suffering from depression, coping with a painful breakup, or something else, prayer has always been one of the most effective ways to help people. The Lord will hear the prayers for our friends. Trust in His infinite wisdom.

Do you have a friend in crisis? Are you worried about their health? Share your thoughts with God.

Reflections and thoughts

_____

_____

_____

_____

_____

_____

_____

I am grateful for

_____

_____

_____

_____

_____

Things on my mind

_____

_____

_____

_____

_____

Prayer requests

_____

_____

_____

_____

_____

Prayers answered

_____

_____

_____

_____

_____

Praying for others

Let nothing be done through selfish ambition or conceit, but in lowliness of mind let each esteem others better than himself. Let each of you look out not only for his own interests but also for the interests of others.

Philippians 2:3-4

PRAYING FOR LEADERS

Ask the Lord to watch over them and lead them into hope and blessing. Ask him to help them to be wise, brave, and right-minded. A true leader should uplift others and act with integrity. He/she is willing to take advice and receive constructive criticism. True leaders are respected if they respect others.

Have you taken the time to pray for your leaders recently? What are the things you want to say to God?

Reflections and thoughts

_____

_____

_____

_____

_____

_____

_____

I am grateful for

_____

_____

_____

_____

_____

Things on my mind

_____

_____

_____

_____

_____

Prayer requests

_____

_____

_____

_____

_____

Prayers answered

_____

_____

_____

_____

_____

Praying for others

See that no one repays anyone evil for evil, but always seek to do good to one another and to everyone.

Thessalonians 5:15

PRAY FOR THE DIFFICULT PEOPLE IN YOUR LIFE

The Holy book tells us to love all humanity. However, it is easy to love our family and friends, but it is not easy to love someone who is hard to love. Do not worry, the Lord knows your struggles. Your task is to pray for them and do not expect anything in return. Be patient, give grace and empathy. Simply put, don't make a big show of it.

Who do you struggle to love? A co-worker? A rebellious teen?

Reflections and thoughts

_____
_____
_____
_____
_____
_____
_____
_____

I am grateful for

_____
_____
_____
_____
_____
_____

Things on my mind

_____
_____
_____
_____
_____
_____

Prayer requests

_____
_____
_____
_____
_____

Prayers answered

_____
_____
_____
_____
_____

Praying for others

But I say to you, love your enemies and pray for those who persecute you.

Matthew 5:44

PRAYING FOR YOUR ENEMIES

Pray for them and God will turn their hostility into empathy and understanding. Ask God to help you forgive them. Do good to them, bless them all the time, and thank God for them. He will give them a reason to not just feel sincere regret but love again. We are all God's children. Look at them through God's eyes.

What do you see? Pain? Misery? Write down below your thoughts and ask God to bless them.

Reflections and thoughts

_____

_____

_____

_____

_____

_____

_____

_____

I am grateful for

_____

_____

_____

_____

_____

_____

Things on my mind

_____

_____

_____

_____

_____

_____

Prayer requests

_____

_____

_____

_____

_____

_____

Prayers answered

_____

_____

_____

_____

_____

_____

Praying for others

We will show mercy to the poor and not miss an opportunity to do acts of kindness for others, for these are the true sacrifices that delight God's heart.

Hebrews 13:16

HOW TO PRAY FOR SOMEONE

With God, all things are possible. God is all-wise by its nature and there is nothing hard for Him to do. He is able to help a person without violating their freedom. Devine intelligence can do many things to influence people to point them in the right direction, without forcing them. Thus, you do not have to worry about the ethics of your prayers for another person.

Ask the Lord to help others freely. What will you say to God?

Reflections and thoughts

_____

_____

_____

_____

_____

_____

_____

I am grateful for

_____

_____

_____

_____

_____

_____

Things on my mind

_____

_____

_____

_____

_____

_____

Prayer requests

_____

_____

_____

_____

_____

_____

Prayers answered

_____

_____

_____

_____

_____

_____

Praying for health

Do not get drunk on wine, which leads to debauchery. Instead, be filled with the Spirit.

Ephesians 5:18

DEVELOPING GOOD HEALTH HABITS

Human health has six dimensions – physical, emotional, social, intellectual, occupational, and spiritual. There are many healthy habits that cover all of these dimensions. They include drinking plenty of water, exercising, keeping your balance, being mindful, and so on. Good health habits are important because they are the key to living well and long.

Fortunately, God has your back. Ask your Heavenly Father to help you with good health habits.

Reflections and thoughts

_____
_____
_____
_____
_____
_____
_____

I am grateful for

_____
_____
_____
_____
_____
_____

Things on my mind

_____
_____
_____
_____
_____
_____

Prayer requests

_____
_____
_____
_____
_____
_____

Prayers answered

_____
_____
_____
_____
_____

Praying for health

Don't you know that you yourselves are God's temple and that God's Spirit dwells in your midst? If anyone destroys God's temple, God will destroy that person; for God's temple is sacred, and you together are that temple.

Corinthians 3:16-17

PRAYING FOR A STRONG BODY

Your body is a temple. What does it mean? To the Israelites, people of the Ancient World, the temple was their sacred meeting place with the Lord. In fact, God makes us His temple; we should keep this fact in mind

Are you worried about your body? Have you shared your concerns with God? Ask God to bless you with a strong body so that you will have a powerful defense against illness and injury.

Reflections and thoughts

_____

_____

_____

_____

_____

_____

_____

_____

I am grateful for

_____

_____

_____

_____

_____

_____

Things on my mind

_____

_____

_____

_____

_____

_____

Prayer requests

_____

_____

_____

_____

_____

Prayers answered

_____

_____

_____

_____

_____

Praying for health

Dear friend, I pray that you may enjoy good health and that all may go well with you, even as your soul is getting along well.

3 John 1:2

PRAYING FOR A STRONG IMMUNE SYSTEM

Do not put yourself in an environment that puts you at a higher risk of losing your willpower. Avoid temptations such as junk food, soda, and too much sugar. Cook your own food, take vitamins and minerals, make sure to drink good-quality water, make exercise a habit, get a good night's sleep.

If self-discipline feels difficult to you, ask the Holy Spirit to reveal the secret to self-control and help you develop good habits.

Reflections and thoughts

_____
_____
_____
_____
_____
_____
_____

I am grateful for

_____
_____
_____
_____
_____
_____

Things on my mind

_____
_____
_____
_____
_____
_____

Prayer requests

_____
_____
_____
_____
_____

Prayers answered

_____
_____
_____
_____
_____

Praying for health

Beloved, I pray that all may go well with you and that you may be in good health, as it goes well with your soul.

John 1:2

ACHIEVING DIVINE HEALTH

Knowing that God has already made us perfect in health is something that can calm your mind and fill your soul with joy. Your divine health comes from God. After all, God's divine health is your health too. Remember, you are God's child! God wants His children to be healthy and content. Developing a healthy relationship with the Word of God and the Holy Spirit will supernaturally sustain your body in perfect divine health.

The exercise for this week is – I am struggling with… Write it down.

Reflections and thoughts

_____

_____

_____

_____

_____

_____

_____

I am grateful for

_____

_____

_____

_____

_____

_____

Things on my mind

_____

_____

_____

_____

_____

_____

Prayer requests

_____

_____

_____

_____

_____

Prayers answered

_____

_____

_____

_____

_____

Praying for health

Do not be anxious about anything, but in every situation, by prayer and petition, with thanksgiving, present your requests to God. And the peace of God, which transcends all understanding, will guard your hearts and your minds in Christ Jesus.

Philippians 4:6-7

PRAYING FOR GOOD MENTAL HEALTH

Do you notice feeling anxiety, worry, stress, sadness, or other "negative" emotions? Take a deep breath and pause to consider your response. Some ways to protect your mental health include helping others, keeping a gratitude journal, and praying. Studies have shown that prayer can reduce levels of anxiety and stress, as well as prevent depression.

How are you feeling today? Ask God to help you stay calm and grateful in stressful situations.

Reflections and thoughts

_____
_____
_____
_____
_____
_____
_____

I am grateful for

_____
_____
_____
_____
_____
_____

Things on my mind

_____
_____
_____
_____
_____
_____

Prayer requests

_____
_____
_____
_____
_____
_____

Prayers answered

_____
_____
_____
_____
_____
_____

Praying for health

For the mind set on the flesh is death, but the mind set on the Spirit is life and peace.

Romans 8:6

PRAYING FOR GOOD SPIRITUAL HEALTH

Ask God, "How can I be of most service to others? How can I be of most service to you?" Researchers have found that prayer can calm your nervous system and eliminate negative emotions, turning them into acceptance, gratefulness, and stillness. It strengthens a sense of connection with the higher power of the Holy Spirit. Remember, prayer is only likely to have health benefits if you are open to it!

Is something bothering you? Do you want to ask God for something?

Reflections and thoughts

_____

_____

_____

_____

_____

_____

_____

_____

I am grateful for

_____

_____

_____

_____

_____

Things on my mind

_____

_____

_____

_____

_____

Prayer requests

_____

_____

_____

_____

_____

Prayers answered

_____

_____

_____

_____

Praying for health

Pleasant words are a honeycomb,
Sweet to the soul and healing to the bones.

Proverbs 16:24

THE HEALING POWER OF PRAYER

The Lord wants us to be whole and content, not just in our spirit but also in our human body. God will comfort you in suffering whatever pain you face. He can give you the confidence to put your complete trust in His mighty hands. Remember, healing is coming.

Whether you pray for yourself or your friend, turn to God with all your heart and soul. Do you have certain health issues? What will you say to God?

Reflections and thoughts

_____

_____

_____

_____

_____

_____

_____

I am grateful for

_____

_____

_____

_____

_____

_____

Things on my mind

_____

_____

_____

_____

_____

_____

Prayer requests

_____

_____

_____

_____

_____

_____

Prayers answered

_____

_____

_____

_____

_____

_____

Praying for love

My command is this: Love each other as I have loved you.

John 15:12

GOD IS LOVE

A key part of the journey to finding true love is faith. When you are searching for love in this world, keep in mind that God's love is unconditional and infinite. God's love is perfect. God is love. Our ability to love is enabled through His love. God is light. It brightens up our world, revealing the truth.

We are loved by God. How much do you love God?

Reflections and thoughts

_____
_____
_____
_____
_____
_____
_____

I am grateful for

_____
_____
_____
_____
_____

Things on my mind

_____
_____
_____
_____
_____

Prayer requests

_____
_____
_____
_____
_____

Prayers answered

_____
_____
_____
_____
_____

Praying for love

But you, my Lord, are a God of compassion and mercy; you are very patient and full of faithful love.

Psalm 86:15

RESTING IN GOD'S LOVE

We are here in the name of love. Ask God to bless you with love so you can love as He loves us and show tolerance and patience. If you believe in God and follow His teachings, you can sleep peacefully, knowing you are never alone. So, rest from worrying about the future and beating yourself up over wrong choices. Just remember – the Lord is always with you.

Do you struggle with the feeling you are not doing enough for the Lord, Jesus Christ, and this world? Share your fears and worries with God and ask Him to help you overcome them.

Reflections and thoughts

_____

_____

_____

_____

_____

_____

_____

_____

I am grateful for

_____

_____

_____

_____

_____

_____

Things on my mind

_____

_____

_____

_____

_____

_____

Prayer requests

_____

_____

_____

_____

_____

Prayers answered

_____

_____

_____

_____

_____

Praying for love

See what kind of love the Father has given to us in that we should be called God's children, and that is what we are! Because the world didn't recognize him, it doesn't recognize us.

John 3:1

HELP ME TO LOVE MYSELF

A parent loves their child. A good parent loves all their kids equally. You are one of God's children, whom He loves the same way. God wants you to love yourself. It is such a blessing! He has created you perfectly in His image; thus, God does not want you to go through your lives filled with disappointment and insecurities about yourselves.

Imagine knowing that your beloved ones feel incapable of loving themselves. You can feel their despair, loneliness, and sadness, right?! How desperately would you want to tell them that they're loved?

Reflections and thoughts

_____

_____

_____

_____

_____

_____

_____

I am grateful for

_____

_____

_____

_____

_____

_____

Things on my mind

_____

_____

_____

_____

_____

_____

Prayer requests

_____

_____

_____

_____

_____

_____

Prayers answered

_____

_____

_____

_____

_____

_____

Praying for love

Love is patient, love is kind. It does not envy, it does not boast, it is not proud. It does not dishonor others, it is not self-seeking, it is not easily angered, it keeps no record of wrongs. Love does not delight in evil but rejoices with the truth. It always protects, always trusts, always hopes, always perseveres. Love never fails…

Corinthians 13:4-8

HEAL MY HEART PRAYER

If you've suffered a lot of pain in your love relationship, it is hard to move on. We've all been there. However, God is our healer; try to find strength in Him. Remember, in any relationship, you have God's love on your side. If someone broke your heart, you do not have to fight this alone. If you deeply desire to have someone in your life again, after all the struggles and hardships, pray to God and He will hear your cry!

You're deserving of love. God teaches you to appreciate yourself for whom you are. Take time to make a list of 5 to 10 things that you think you deserve.

Reflections and thoughts

_____

_____

_____

_____

_____

_____

_____

I am grateful for

_____

_____

_____

_____

_____

_____

Things on my mind

_____

_____

_____

_____

_____

_____

Prayer requests

_____

_____

_____

_____

_____

_____

Prayers answered

_____

_____

_____

_____

_____

_____

Praying for love

As soon as he had finished speaking to Saul, the soul of Jonathan was knit to the soul of David, and Jonathan loved him as his own soul.

Samuel 18:1

SEARCHING FOR SOULMATE AND SOUL CONNECTION

Today is the most important moment in your life. When you ask the Lord specifically to be a part of your life, now, in the present moment, then you are more likely to keep His divine love in each moment. If you haven't found your soulmate yet, ask God to help you recognize them when you finally meet "The One". Pray to heal potential love wounds. If you are lucky to have them in your life, pray for one another. Do not take this God-honoring relationship for granted; it is God's reward!

Ask God to fill you with His sacred presence. Ask for a blessing. What else would you say?

Reflections and thoughts

_____

_____

_____

_____

_____

_____

_____

I am grateful for

_____

_____

_____

_____

_____

_____

Things on my mind

_____

_____

_____

_____

_____

_____

Prayer requests

_____

_____

_____

_____

_____

Prayers answered

_____

_____

_____

_____

_____

Praying for love

But because of the temptation to sexual immorality, each man should have his own wife and each woman her own husband.

Corinthians 7:2

PRAY FOR YOUR MARRIAGE OR ROMANTIC RELATIONSHIP

Our families are vulnerable in this chaotic world. While a romantic relationship can be full of fun, it can also be full of pressure. Our commitments to marriage vows and promises are under constant assault. God understands your worries and fears.

Pray for guidance in your relationship. Pray that you will be a better wife or partner. What will you say to God?

Reflections and thoughts

_____
_____
_____
_____
_____
_____
_____
_____

I am grateful for

_____
_____
_____
_____
_____
_____

Things on my mind

_____
_____
_____
_____
_____
_____

Prayer requests

_____
_____
_____
_____
_____
_____

Prayers answered

_____
_____
_____
_____
_____
_____

Praying for love

We love because he first loved us.

John 4:19 E

LOVE MEANS GIVING

Give what you want to receive. If you want to receive love, give love. God teaches us that love is about giving a lot and expecting less. It is the key to happiness in love! Remember, God willingly sacrifices His only Son to save us; ask God to help you entrust your heart in someone's hands. Trust God first and you will experience real love!

What will you give to your Heavenly Father? What will you give to your beloved one?

Reflections and thoughts

_____

_____

_____

_____

_____

_____

_____

_____

I am grateful for

_____

_____

_____

_____

_____

Things on my mind

_____

_____

_____

_____

_____

Prayer requests

_____

_____

_____

_____

_____

Prayers answered

_____

_____

_____

_____

_____

Praying for wisdom

And it is my prayer that your love may abound more and more, with knowledge and all discernment, so that you may approve what is excellent, and so be pure and blameless for the day of Christ.

Philippians 1:9-10

PRAY FOR GUIDANCE

God is your Good Shepherd; He desires that we follow the path of happiness. When you pray for God's direction and discernment, you can rest assured that God will provide directions! Do not worry about tomorrow, do not rush your day without asking God for guidance!

Do your best to get wisdom. You have everything you need inside you to do so. Ask God to give you clear guidance in life.

Reflections and thoughts

_____

_____

_____

_____

_____

_____

_____

I am grateful for

Things on my mind

_____

_____

_____

_____

_____

_____

Prayer requests

Prayers answered

_____

_____

_____

_____

_____

_____

Praying for wisdom

Show me your ways, LORD, teach me your paths. Guide me in your truth and teach me, for you are God my Savior, and my hope is in you all day long.

Psalm 25:4-5

PRAYING FOR DECISION MAKING

When you need to make a decision, if you feel undecided and confused, you can't rely only on your experience or on someone's advice. You actually need peace in your mind and heart. Do not worry, you can tap into the glory of God by faith! The Holy Spirit guides us all in our life adventures. When you ask for God's wisdom, it is very important to trust Him. He will choose the very best path for you.

If you make decisions according to God's will, everything will be perfect. Imagine you already made your decision. God speaks through your feelings. What did you hear?

Reflections and thoughts

_____

_____

_____

_____

_____

_____

_____

I am grateful for

_____

_____

_____

_____

_____

_____

Things on my mind

_____

_____

_____

_____

_____

_____

Prayer requests

_____

_____

_____

_____

_____

Prayers answered

_____

_____

_____

_____

_____

Praying for wisdom

For God speaks in one way, and in two, though man does not perceive it. In a dream, in a vision of the night, when deep sleep falls on men, while they slumber on their beds.

Job 33:14-15

PRAYING FOR WISDOM IN DIFFICULT TIMES

Remember, wisdom (not knowledge) will get you through tough times. What to do to receive answers from God in difficult times? God always hears your prayers and His plans are always better than yours. There are clear signs God is speaking to you. This can take different forms; God speaks through other people, visions, dreams, songs, animals, and his words.

Calm your mind in stressful times and breath; bring yourself into God's presence. Try to be calm and listen to what God is trying to tell you.

Reflections and thoughts

_____

_____

_____

_____

_____

_____

_____

I am grateful for

_____

_____

_____

_____

_____

Things on my mind

_____

_____

_____

_____

_____

Prayer requests

_____

_____

_____

_____

Prayers answered

_____

_____

_____

_____

Praying for wisdom

And so, from the day we heard, we have not ceased to pray for you, asking that you may be filled with the knowledge of his will in all spiritual wisdom and understanding.

Colossians 1:9-10

PRAYING FOR WISDOM IN GOOD TIMES

True wisdom is something God offers constantly. It is a precious spiritual gift, which can be manifested in pure hearts and righteous lives. Wisdom doesn't end with knowledge; it is constantly expanding and deepening. If you want to experience the fullness of God's wisdom, you must prepare your spirit for the glory of God. Look for God's wisdom, pray for His glory, and live in God's rest.

Did you know that the wisdom of God is available to you 24/7?

Reflections and thoughts

_____
_____
_____
_____
_____
_____
_____

I am grateful for

_____
_____
_____
_____
_____

Things on my mind

_____
_____
_____
_____
_____

Prayer requests

_____
_____
_____
_____
_____

Prayers answered

_____
_____
_____
_____
_____

Praying for wisdom

When pride comes, then comes disgrace, but with humility comes wisdom.

Proverbs 11:2

PRAYING FOR WISDOM AT WORK

A successful businesswoman always has a goal and a purpose. She thinks before speaking, listens to others carefully, and keeps her power in every situation. A wise woman in business balances self-interest with the collective good, making the most of every opportunity. When you are not sure how to act at work, turn to God for guidance.

For instance, I am struggling with… Write it down.

Reflections and thoughts

_____

_____

_____

_____

_____

_____

_____

I am grateful for

_____

_____

_____

_____

_____

Things on my mind

_____

_____

_____

_____

_____

Prayer requests

_____

_____

_____

_____

Prayers answered

_____

_____

_____

_____

Praying for wisdom

If any of you lacks wisdom, let him ask God, who gives generously to all without reproach, and it will be given him.

James 1:5

PRAYING FOR UNDERSTANDING OTHERS

When you turn to the Lord, you are able to sense the power of His love and wisdom. Turning to His infinite wisdom for guidance is something that you can do every day. Even if you are feeling stuck and confused in relationships right now, God is still God. He is still your strength, your love, and your divine wisdom.

God knows you and the people around you. Ask Him to fill you with wisdom in your relationships. What would you say?

Reflections and thoughts

_____

_____

_____

_____

_____

_____

_____

I am grateful for

_____

_____

_____

_____

_____

_____

Things on my mind

_____

_____

_____

_____

_____

_____

Prayer requests

_____

_____

_____

_____

_____

_____

Prayers answered

_____

_____

_____

_____

_____

Praying for wisdom

The wise woman builds her house, but with her own hands the foolish one tears hers down.

Proverbs 14:1

LOOK FOR WISDOM
IN PARENTING

Children are one of the most precious gifts from God. If you want your children to grow up to be independent and caring adults, you should be a confident and wise mother. You need to have the lead role in the spiritual lives of your children. Your goal is to lay a spiritual foundation in them, so they will always look at God as their Father. By embracing activities such as prayer and putting them into daily practice, you will build their spiritual strength.

Take a deep breath and with a humble heart, ask God for protection and safety. Ask God for his powerful presence and purpose in parenting.

Reflections and thoughts

_____

_____

_____

_____

_____

_____

_____

I am grateful for

_____

_____

_____

_____

_____

_____

Things on my mind

_____

_____

_____

_____

_____

_____

Prayer requests

_____

_____

_____

_____

_____

_____

Prayers answered

_____

_____

_____

_____

_____

_____

Praying for wisdom

For the Lord gives wisdom; from his mouth come knowledge and understanding.

Proverbs 2:6

A FULL UNDERSTANDING OF GOD'S WORD

In this uncertain world, it is not easy to stay grounded. However, God has your back. The Word of God has amazing, supernatural power. However, it only works for those who believe. If you are looking for wisdom, you can't trust everything you hear on the Internet, from your teachers, authorities, and scientists. But God's Word is entirely true! This is the wisdom that comes from being known and loved by God!

Pray for a full understanding of the Word of God. What will you say to God?

Reflections and thoughts

_____

_____

_____

_____

_____

_____

_____

_____

I am grateful for

_____

_____

_____

_____

_____

Things on my mind

_____

_____

_____

_____

_____

Prayer requests

_____

_____

_____

_____

_____

Prayers answered

_____

_____

_____

_____

_____

Praying for conficence & humility

For the Lord will be your confidence and will keep your foot from being caught.

Proverbs 3:26

CONFIDENCE IN GOD

Trusting in the Lord is the key component of any prayer. One of the best ways to build a relationship with God is through prayers. God is who He says He is. If you turn to God and receive the blessings, there is nothing that we can't do. Everything is possible! Miracles happen!

Remember, trust in God and He will help you! If you have any concerns, write them down.

Reflections and thoughts

_____

_____

_____

_____

_____

_____

_____

I am grateful for

_____

_____

_____

_____

_____

Things on my mind

_____

_____

_____

_____

_____

Prayer requests

_____

_____

_____

_____

Prayers answered

_____

_____

_____

_____

Praying for conficence & humility

Therefore, do not throw away your confidence, which has a great reward.

Hebrews 10:35

PRAYING FOR SELF-CONFIDENCE

When you're feeling worthless, remember – God created you with a purpose. Your purpose is to create good things for the Lord and this world. From the very beginning, that's the power of the confidence we have in God. And so it is. Just rest in this Truth.

How does a lack of confidence affect your life? Ask God to give you more confidence in life.

Reflections and thoughts

_____
_____
_____
_____
_____
_____
_____
_____

I am grateful for

_____
_____
_____
_____
_____

Things on my mind

_____
_____
_____
_____
_____

Prayer requests

_____
_____
_____
_____
_____

Prayers answered

_____
_____
_____
_____
_____

Praying for conficence & humility

But the fruit of the Spirit is love, joy, peace, patience, kindness, goodness, faithfulness.

Galatians 5:22

LOOK FOR THE FRUIT OF THE SPIRIT

Do not be afraid. Pray through. And most importantly, believe in His plan. Ask God for the Fruits of the Holy Spirit. They include love, peace, patience, kindness, joy, goodness, faithfulness, self-control, and gentleness.

Spend some time talking to the Lord. Tell Him your worries and troubles. Ask Him for the Holy Spirit's presence. What will you say?

Reflections and thoughts

_____

_____

_____

_____

_____

_____

_____

_____

I am grateful for

_____

_____

_____

_____

_____

_____

Things on my mind

_____

_____

_____

_____

_____

_____

Prayer requests

_____

_____

_____

_____

_____

Prayers answered

_____

_____

_____

_____

_____

Praying for conficence & humility

Have I not commanded you? Be strong and courageous. Do not be frightened, and do not be dismayed, for the Lord your God is with you wherever you go.

Joshua 1:9

PRAYING FOR COURAGE

Whether you are worried about your job or family, there are times when we feel afraid and scared of the unknown; there are times when we may need confidence and courage. Praying for courage can help you walk in faith on your path. Believe that God has a plan for you; it will give you courage for the future!

Remember, praying doesn't have to be predetermined and complicated. God understands simple words. In fact, He understands our feelings. Do you want to ask God for courage and confidence?

Reflections and thoughts

_____

_____

_____

_____

_____

_____

_____

I am grateful for

_____

_____

_____

_____

_____

Things on my mind

_____

_____

_____

_____

_____

Prayer requests

_____

_____

_____

_____

_____

_____

Prayers answered

_____

_____

_____

_____

_____

Praying for confidence & humility

Fear not, for I am with you; be not dismayed, for I am your God; I will strengthen you, I will help you, I will uphold you with my righteous right hand.

Isaiah 41:10

PRAYING FOR STRENGTH

Are you looking for peace in the middle of big life changes and decisions? Praying to the Lord to embolden you for these situations is the key to confidence and success. Do not worry, God will show you strengths you never even knew you had!

If you feel mentally and emotionally weak, turn to your Heavenly Father and ask Him for strength. What will you say?

Reflections and thoughts

_____

_____

_____

_____

_____

_____

_____

_____

I am grateful for

_____

_____

_____

_____

_____

Things on my mind

_____

_____

_____

_____

_____

Prayer requests

_____

_____

_____

_____

_____

Prayers answered

_____

_____

_____

_____

Praying for conficence & humility

For you created my inmost being; you knit me together in my mother's womb.
I praise you because I am fearfully and wonderfully made; your works are wonderful,
I know that full well.

Psalm 139:13–14

KNOWING YOUR WORTH

If you feel unworthy of the good things in life, remember – you were wonderfully made by an Almighty God! It means that you can't be a mistake, just the opposite! God created you just the way you are on purpose. In fact, He does everything on purpose. Therefore, walk with your head held high and be happy with yourself!

Everything is already inside you. Pray that God will fill you with a sense of self-worth. Write in your own words.

Reflections and thoughts

_____
_____
_____
_____
_____
_____
_____
_____

I am grateful for

_____
_____
_____
_____
_____
_____

Things on my mind

_____
_____
_____
_____
_____
_____

Prayer requests

_____
_____
_____
_____
_____

Prayers answered

_____
_____
_____
_____
_____

Praying for conficence & humility

Therefore, as God's chosen people, holy and dearly loved, clothe yourselves with compassion, kindness, humility, gentleness, and patience.

Colossians 3:12

PRAYING FOR HUMILITY

Before being proud and honored, a woman must first be humble. If you are grateful for all that you have, knowing that you have gained nothing but your own life. Do not walk in pride and arrogance; walk in God's truth and honor Him in humility. Remember, you are being fully accepted by God; You are accepted for who you are.

Be honest with yourself. Be honest with God. Share your thoughts with God.

Reflections and thoughts

_____
_____
_____
_____
_____
_____
_____
_____

I am grateful for

_____
_____
_____
_____
_____
_____

Things on my mind

_____
_____
_____
_____
_____
_____

Prayer requests

_____
_____
_____
_____
_____
_____

Prayers answered

_____
_____
_____
_____
_____
_____

Praying for conficence & humility

And this is the confidence that we have toward him, that if we ask anything according to his will he hears us.

1 John 5:14

BALANCING CONFIDENCE AND HUMILITY

The greatest women in history are all women of honesty, integrity, and humility. Confidence can help you recognize your strengths and treat yourself with kindness and compassion. Humility can make you less self-focused and more focused on those around you, those in need. In fact, confidence and humility are mutually reinforcing. Showing confidence can induce humility in you; humble people show high self-esteem and appreciation to others.

Do you have any troubles balancing confidence and humility? Ask God for help, using your own words.

Reflections and thoughts

_____

_____

_____

_____

_____

_____

_____

I am grateful for

_____

_____

_____

_____

_____

_____

Things on my mind

_____

_____

_____

_____

_____

_____

Prayer requests

_____

_____

_____

_____

_____

_____

Prayers answered

_____

_____

_____

_____

_____

_____

Praying for gratefulness & mercy

Rejoice always, pray continually, give thanks in all circumstances; for this is God's will for you in Christ Jesus.

Thessalonians 5:16-18

THANK YOU FOR CARING ABOUT MY LIFE

Knowing how to express gratitude to your Heavenly Father through prayers is an essential part of your relationship with God. Whether you are recovering from a certain tragedy or illness, let Him know how much His effort meant to you. Remember, God is involved in every detail of your life. And so, it is. Sit back and rest in this Truth.

Thank God in prayer. Thank God for prayer.

Reflections and thoughts

_____

_____

_____

_____

_____

_____

_____

I am grateful for

_____

_____

_____

_____

_____

_____

Things on my mind

_____

_____

_____

_____

_____

_____

Prayer requests

_____

_____

_____

_____

_____

_____

Prayers answered

_____

_____

_____

_____

_____

_____

Praying for gratefulness & mercy

Oh, give thanks to the LORD, for He is good; for His steadfast love endures forever!

Chronicles 16:34

THANK YOU FOR CREATING ME WITH PURPOSE

Finding your purpose is not the easiest thing in the world. However, knowing that God created you with purpose can set your mind free. Knowing that you play a unique role in each step of your story is a precious gift from God. You can use prayer to thank God for creating you with all your flaws and virtues. Remember – you are God's masterpiece.

From simple prayers to serious devotion, there are many ways to give thanks and develop gratefulness to God. What is your favorite way to thank God?

Reflections and thoughts

_____
_____
_____
_____
_____
_____
_____
_____

I am grateful for

_____
_____
_____
_____
_____
_____

Things on my mind

_____
_____
_____
_____
_____
_____

Prayer requests

_____
_____
_____
_____
_____
_____

Prayers answered

_____
_____
_____
_____
_____
_____

Praying for gratefulness & mercy

Out of his fullness, we have all received grace in place of grace already given.

John 1:16

PRAY THAT YOU REMEMBER GOD'S GRACE FOR YOU

Remember ¬– whatever you ask in prayer, it will be yours. But what's the catch? You should believe that you will receive it and that you deserve God's grace.

If you have fallen on hard times, just take a breath and pray that you remember God's grace always and forever. Pray with your own words and rely on His mercy. Pour out your heart and listen to God's Word. What did you hear?

Reflections and thoughts

_____
_____
_____
_____
_____
_____
_____
_____

I am grateful for

_____
_____
_____
_____
_____
_____
_____

Things on my mind

_____
_____
_____
_____
_____
_____
_____

Prayer requests

_____
_____
_____
_____
_____
_____
_____

Prayers answered

_____
_____
_____
_____
_____
_____
_____

Praying for gratefulness & mercy

I will give thanks to you, Lord, with all my heart;
I will tell of all your wonderful deeds.

Psalm 9:1

PRAYING FOR A HEART OF GRATITUDE

Cultivating a heart of gratitude is one of the essential components of a happy life. When you lack gratitude, you are not allowing yourself to receive God's grace and wisdom. Then, you have feelings of emptiness and a lack of meaning in your life. Do not worry; God is much more patient with every person than they can even imagine.

A heart of gratitude is one of the most important things you should include in your daily prayers. Ask for a heart of gratitude. Pray for others. Thank God. What will you say?

Reflections and thoughts

_____

_____

_____

_____

_____

_____

_____

I am grateful for

_____

_____

_____

_____

_____

_____

Things on my mind

_____

_____

_____

_____

_____

_____

Prayer requests

_____

_____

_____

_____

_____

_____

Prayers answered

_____

_____

_____

_____

_____

_____

Praying for gratefulness & mercy

Let us then with confidence draw near to the throne of grace, that we may receive mercy and find grace to help in time of need.

Hebrews 4:16

PRAYING FOR FAITHFULNESS IN GOD'S MERCY

We all have doubts. It's completely natural and normal. It is also natural that we do not understand the world's true nature. Only God understands it. God's power surpasses any human knowing and acting. God is always by your side with His infinite mercy.

God is listening to you. Pray for a faithful heart. Thank God for a faithful heart!

Reflections and thoughts

_____
_____
_____
_____
_____
_____
_____
_____

I am grateful for

_____
_____
_____
_____
_____
_____
_____

Things on my mind

_____
_____
_____
_____
_____
_____
_____

Prayer requests

_____
_____
_____
_____
_____
_____

Prayers answered

_____
_____
_____
_____
_____
_____

Praying for gratefulness & mercy

Praise the LORD, my soul; all my inmost being, praise His holy name. Praise the LORD, my soul, and forget not all His benefits — who forgives all your sins and heals all your diseases, who redeems your life from the pit and crowns you with love and compassion.

Psalm 103:1-4

PRAISE AND THANKSGIVING

The simplest way to praise God is to pray to Him. You can do this anywhere and at any time. What is most important is that it comes from your heart. Thanksgiving is to show gratitude to God for all the things that He has done for you. In fact, praise is more than words and it comes from highly developed faith. Remember, it is important to praise God at any time, even if you're currently going through troublesome times.

You can thank God for giving you breath, for guidance, for love. Continue a sequence…

Reflections and thoughts

_____

_____

_____

_____

_____

_____

_____

I am grateful for

_____

_____

_____

_____

_____

_____

Things on my mind

_____

_____

_____

_____

_____

_____

Prayer requests

_____

_____

_____

_____

_____

_____

Prayers answered

_____

_____

_____

_____

_____

_____

Praying for gratefulness & mercy

Blessed are the pure in heart, for they shall see God.

Matthew 5:8

PRAYING FOR PURITY

If you need a little help to get into the right mindset, turn to God's mercy and purity. Pure water is free from additives. A pure heart is free from negative emotions. Spiritual purity comes as a result of believing that God made you perfect and fully loved.

As you seek God in your life, ask Him to cleanse your mind, heart, and soul. Ask God to continue blessing your life.

Reflections and thoughts

_____

_____

_____

_____

_____

_____

_____

I am grateful for

_____

_____

_____

_____

_____

Things on my mind

_____

_____

_____

_____

_____

Prayer requests

_____

_____

_____

_____

_____

Prayers answered

_____

_____

_____

_____

_____